★★★★★

MLB TEAMS

Chicago CUBS

KENNY ABDO

Fly!
An Imprint of Abdo Zoom
abdobooks.com

abdobooks.com

Published by Abdo Zoom, a division of ABDO, P.O. Box 398166, Minneapolis, Minnesota 55439.

Printed in the United States of America, North Mankato, Minnesota.
102025
012026

Photo Credits: Alamy, AP Images, Getty Images, Shutterstock
Production Contributors: Kenny Abdo, Jennie Forsberg, Grace Hansen
Design Contributors: Candice Keimig, Neil Klinepier

Library of Congress Control Number: 2025936772

Publisher's Cataloging-in-Publication Data

Names: Abdo, Kenny, author.
Title: Chicago Cubs / by Kenny Abdo
Description: Minneapolis, Minnesota : Abdo Zoom, 2026 | Series: MLB teams | Includes online resources and index.
Identifiers: ISBN 9798384940135 (lib. bdg.) | ISBN 9798384940890 (ebook) | ISBN 9798384941279 (read-to-me ebook)
Subjects: LCSH: Chicago Cubs (Baseball team)--Juvenile literature. | Baseball teams--Juvenile literature. | Professional sports--Juvenile literature. | Sports franchises--Juvenile literature. | Major League Baseball (Organization)--Juvenile literature.
Classification: DDC 796.357--dc23

Table of CONTENTS

CUBS

Since the late 1800s, the Cubs have made the Windy City a tough place for rivals to breeze through during baseball season!

WRIGLEY FIELD
HOME OF
CHICAGO CUBS
CUBS WIN!
TOYOTA
WELCOME TO THE FRIENDLY CONFINES

From the **Great Cub Curse** to a World Series win, the North Siders have shown that hope in your team should never fade. Even if getting to the top takes 140 years!

BATTER UP!

Founded as the Chicago White Stockings in 1870, the team would become a key piece of the **National League** (**NL**). They played their first game in 1876, showing off their talent on the field. In 1903, the team changed its name to the Cubs.

CHICAGO

The Cubs had a great season in 1906, winning 116 games. The team's strong pitchers, led by Mordecai Brown, helped the Cubs win again and again.

Even though the Cubs lost to the White Sox in the first all-Chicago World Series, it was still one of the best seasons in team history.

The Cubs made a great comeback in 1907 and 1908. The team won back-to-back championships!

Those victories made the Cubs the first Major League Baseball (MLB) team to win two titles in a row.

GRAND SLAMS

In 1910, the Cubs were a powerhouse, finishing the season with 104 wins. However, the team was bested by the Athletics in the World Series, starting a decades-long **drought** for Chicago.

The Cubs had ups and downs over the next few decades. They reached the World Series six times but never came out as champions. The team won **NL pennants** in 1935, 1938, and 1945, giving fans hope with each run.

HIC
HIC

WINTRUST
NATIONAL LEAGUE
CHAMPIONS

After many years without a title, the Cubs' 2016 season became one to remember. They clinched the **NL** Championship Series. The Cubs would go on to end a 108-year World Series **drought** to defeat Cleveland in seven games!

The 2016 victory broke **records** and ended a long-standing curse. Cubs fans celebrated all around Chicago. The championship season earned the Cubs the **Laureus World Team of the Year** award in 2017.

WRIGLEY FIELD
HOME OF
CHICAGO CUBS
WORLD SERIES CHAMPIONS
TOYOTA

Between 2017 and 2025, the Cubs experienced playoff runs and big roster changes. With Pete Crow-Armstrong and Seiya Suzuki leading the way, the Cubs went 92–70 in the 2025 season. They won their first playoff series since 2017 and went on to the **Division** Series.

Though they lost 3–2 to the Brewers, Cubs fans were used to waiting and believing in their team.

HALL OF FAME

Ernie Banks spent his entire career with the Cubs, playing both shortstop and first base. He hit 512 home runs and won two MVP awards. He was **inducted** into the Baseball Hall of Fame in 1977.

CUBS

Ryne Sandberg wowed fans with his strong hitting and great defense. He earned nine Gold Glove awards and played in 10 **All-Star Games**. Sandberg hit 282 home runs and drove in more than 1,000 runs, helping lead the Cubs to the playoffs in 1984. He entered the Baseball Hall of Fame in 2005.

Ron Santo thrilled Cubs fans with his amazing hitting from 1960 to 1973. He was asked to play in nine **All-Star Games** and collected five Gold Glove awards. Santo hit 342 home runs and collected more than 2,200 hits, earning his place in the Baseball Hall of Fame in 2012.

RON SANTO
Empathetic Voice Of The Fans On WGN Radio
For 21 Seasons.
Tireless Fighter, Survivor And Champion

GLOSSARY

All-Star Game – a yearly baseball contest where top players from the AL (American League) and the NL compete against each other.

division – a number of teams grouped together in a sport for competitive purposes.

drought – a long period when a team does not win a major title or playoff series.

Great Cub Curse – also called the "Curse of the Billy Goat," a sports curse that was said to have been placed on the Chicago Cubs in 1945 by Billy Goat Tavern owner William Sianis.

inducted – brought in as a member.

Laureus World Team of the Year – a global sports award given each year to the team with the best performance in any sport.

National League (NL) – one of two 15-team leagues that make up MLB.

pennant – the title achieved by the team that wins its division or league championship.

record – a team's season total of wins and losses; a top achievement by a player or team that no one has done before.

ONLINE RESOURCES

To learn more about the Chicago Cubs, please visit **abdobooklinks.com** or scan this QR code. These links are routinely monitored and updated to provide the most current information available.

INDEX